Mr. Paul
and
Mr. Luecke
Build
Communities

written by
ALICE K. FLANAGAN

photographs by
ROMIE FLANAGAN

Reading Consultant
LINDA CORNWELL
Learning Resource Consultant
Indiana Department of Education

CHILDREN'S PRESS®   *A Division of Grolier Publishing*
New York • London • Hong Kong • Sydney • Danbury, Connecticut

*Special thanks to Mr. Paul and Mr. Luecke
for allowing us to tell their story.*

*To my father, Anthony L. Paul, and my father-in-law, Homer
Lemmons; my wife, Charlene, and our children, Jimmy and
Kimberly; and to all the children who make life fun. —Jim Paul*

*To my father, Lawrence Luecke.
—Jim Luecke*

Visit Children's Press® on the Internet at:
http://publishing.grolier.com

Author's Note: Mr. Luecke's last name is
pronounced LOO-kee

Library of Congress Cataloging-in-Publication Data
Flanagan, Alice K.
   Mr. Paul and Mr. Luecke build communities / written by Alice K.
Flanagan; photographs by Romie Flanagan; reading consultant, Linda
Cornwell, learning resource consultant, Indiana Department of
Education.
      p. cm. – (Our neighborhood)
   Summary: Describes the activities of a real estate developer and a
master carpenter who plan and build new houses in a community.
   ISBN 0-516-21131-5 (lib. bdg.)   0-516-26540-7 (pbk.)
   1. Building—Juvenile literature. [1. Real estate development.
2. Building 3. Occupations.] I. Title. II. Series: Our Neighborhood
(New York, N.Y.)
TH149.F53 1999
690–dc21   98-44690
                                                               CIP
                                                               AC

Photographs ©: Romie Flanagan

Mr. Paul looks out over the land
he has bought. He thinks about
how it will look with streets and
houses on it.

Mr. Paul and his partner,
Mr. Luecke, build communities.

Communities are neighborhoods
where people live and work.

Mr. Paul and Mr. Luecke work together as a team. Mr. Paul does all the planning. He is the developer.

Mr. Luecke builds the house. He is the chief carpenter.

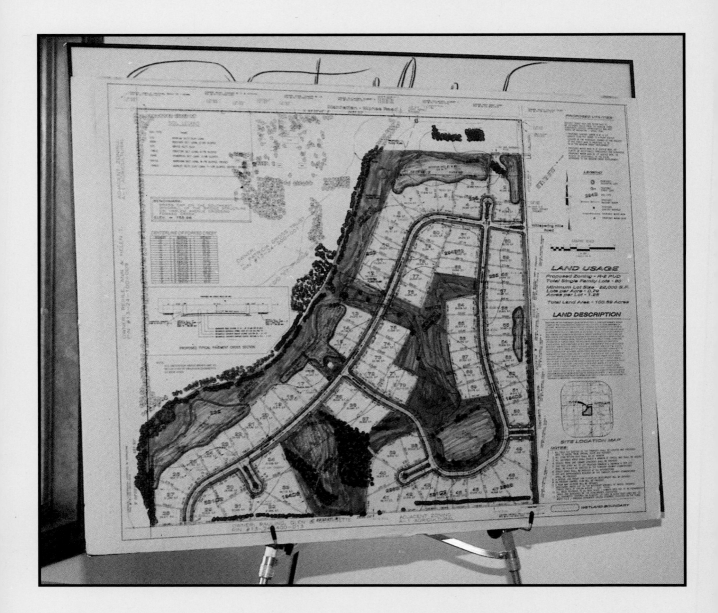

Before Mr. Luecke can build, Mr. Paul must do many things. First, he pays an artist to draw plans of how the community will look.

He takes his plans to the town leaders to get permission to build.

Then, Mr. Paul orders the supplies and hires the workers that Mr. Luecke will need to build the houses.

Mr. Paul meets with each family
who wants to live in the community.
They sign a contract, or agreement,
before their house is built.

Workers prepare the land for the community. They even out the ground and make the roads.

Mr. Luecke digs a large hole for each house in the community. He pours in concrete to make a foundation.

When the concrete dries, it is strong and hard. The house will sit on top of the foundation.

Then, Mr. Luecke builds the wooden frame.

The frame holds up the house and gives it shape.

Mr. Luecke and his helpers build the floors, the walls, and the roof.

They measure, cut, and hammer.

They check the house plans many times. Everything must be done just right.

Next, they nail
sheets of wood
to the outside
of the frame.

They trim the frame with windows and doors.

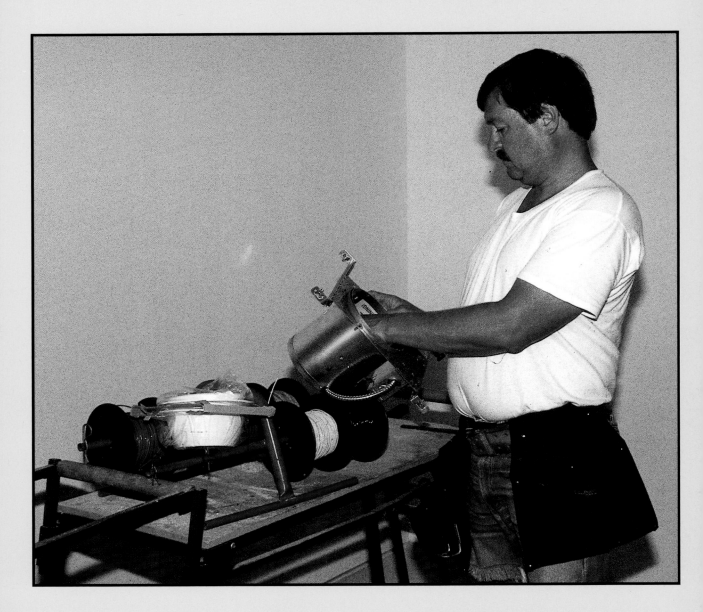

Inside the house, the electricians and plumbers put in the wires and pipes. The painters paint the walls.

Outside, the workers build streets and sidewalks. They will plant trees and grass.

Soon, Mr. Paul and Mr. Luecke will be finished building. Then they will add ponds and lakes for the wildlife.

What a wonderful community
it will be!

Mr. Paul and Mr. Luecke are proud of the communities they build for families.

They do their best to make each new community a beautiful place to live.

Meet the Author
and the Photographer

Alice and Romie Flanagan live in Chicago, Illinois, and have been involved in publishing for many years. Alice is a writer, and Romie is a photographer. As husband and wife, they enjoy working together closely. They hope their books help children learn about the people in their community and how their jobs affect the neighborhood.